Dedications

With love and aloha for the Adorables: Carson, Maren, Samantha, and Taylor
- M.S

Nothing is impossible if you try hard enough.
- A.L.

Published and distributed by

ISLAND HERITAGE®
175 Kahelu Avenue, Unit #4
Mililani, Hawai`i 96789
Orders: (800) 468-2800
Information: (808) 564-8800
Fax: (808) 564-8877
welcometotheislands.com

ISBN: 1-61710-445-0, EAN: 978-1-61710-445-9
First Edition, First Printing—2020
COP 201108

Little Calabash

Written by Margo Leipua'ala Sorenson
Illustrated by Anneth Lagamo

ISLAND HERITAGE®

Little Calabash sat on the shelf way behind all the big calabashes. He sighed. Keoki's mom bustled around the kitchen.

She stirred guava
frosting with spoons,
poured haupia
pudding into bowls,
rolled starfruit cookies
with the rolling pin,
mixed mango cupcakes
with the mixer,
and grated fresh
coconut with the grater.
CHK
CHK
CHK
Everyone in the kitchen was needed
for Keoki's birthday party ...
... everyone but him.

"When will it be my turn?" Little Calabash asked.

"Get a handle on yourself," said the cocoa mug.

"Stop your whining," said the goblet.

"You need to chill out," the refrigerator said, frostily.

"Just because I'm small doesn't mean I'm not special, does it?" Little Calabash asked hopefully.

"You can't beat me," said the mixer.

"Quit trying to stir up trouble," said the wooden spoon.

"But why can't somebody use me too?"
Little Calabash cried.

"Sorry, you're just not big enough," one of the big calabashes said.

Little Calabash felt a tear form.

The coffee pot whispered, "Perk up, kid. You are special. Keep believing in yourself. You'll see!"

"I will?" blurted Little Calabash.
"But - how?"

"Try to keep an open mind,"
said the can opener.

He knew he could be used for something - he just didn't know what it could be.

"How can I be used for the party?" he asked.

"How will they ever find me? I'm stuck in the back of the shelf!"

“You’re straining yourself, kid,” said the colander.

“Go hang out with the chopsticks. Maybe they can pick you up.”

Nothing anyone said was going to stop Little Calabash!

Tipping himself from side-to-side, he carefully wiggled his way from behind all the big calabashes.

He worked himself, inch-by-inch, toward the open cupboard door.

"You need more sizzle, kid," said the frying pan, as Keoki's mom took the pan out of the drawer.

"You're just not as hot as I am," said the toaster.

"You just don't measure up," said the teaspoon.

He had to keep believing, Little Calabash encouraged himself.

Taking a deep breath, he continued wiggling his way forward.

Keoki's mom walked over to the open cupboard. Would she see him? Would she use him?

Not yet. She took two big calabashes off the shelf, instead.

Little Calabash sighed; he began tipping back and forth again, inching himself forward.

"Time to get ready for your birthday party, Keoki," Mom called. Keoki raced into the kitchen.

"Can we put my birthday cupcake into a calabash, and not on a plate?" he asked.

Mom looked at him. "Hmmm," she said. "There aren't enough cupcakes to fill a big calabash."

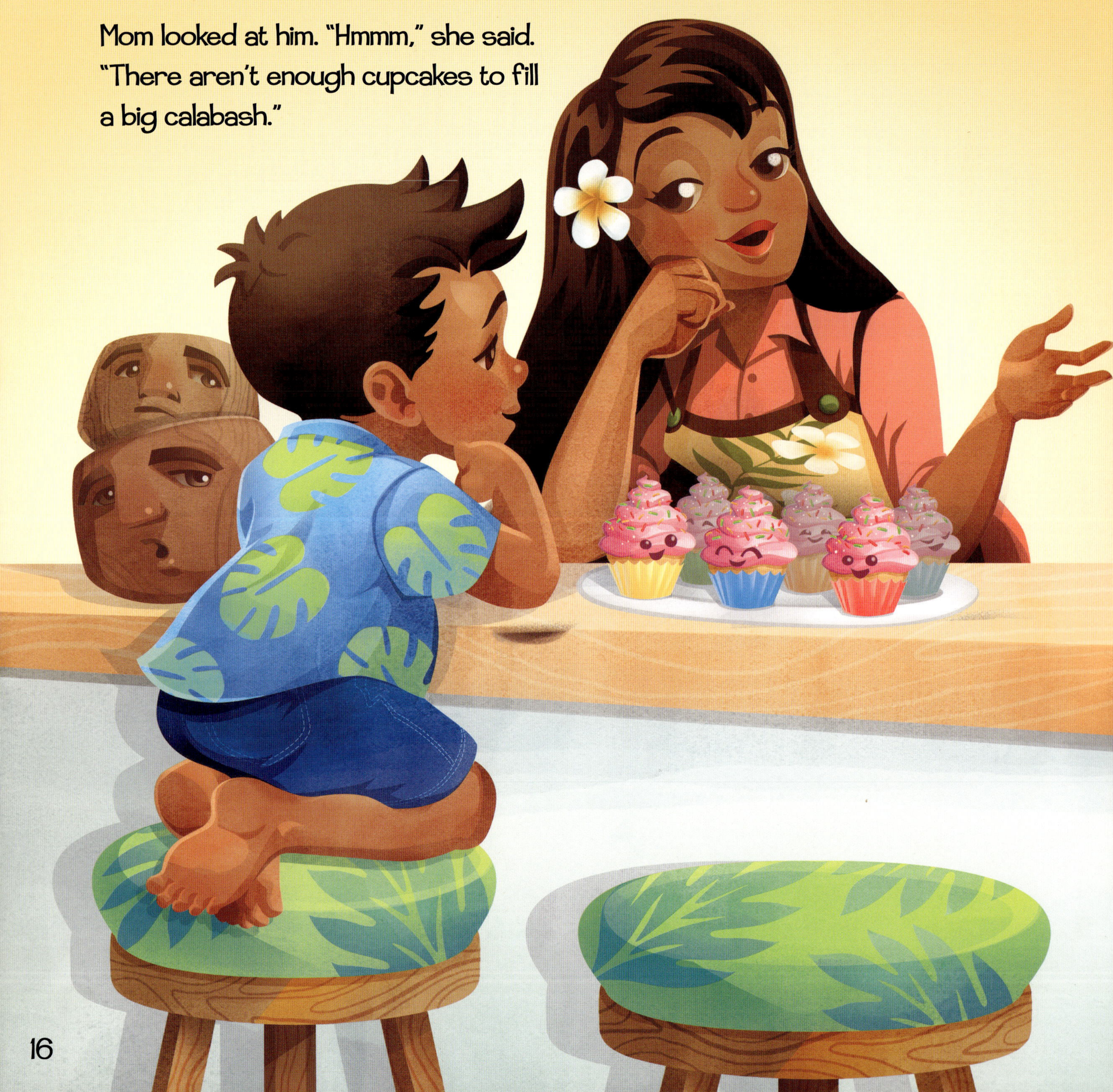

"Don't we have a little calabash, just my size, to fit my cupcake?" Keoki asked.

"Yes! Me! Me!" Little Calabash wanted to shout.

In a last, desperate move, he scooted himself to the very front of the shelf, almost teetering off the edge.

"Maybe it's finally your turn," said the spatula.

Keoki's mom looked at the calabashes on the shelf. "Aha!" she exclaimed.

She picked up Little Calabash and handed him to Keoki. "I'd forgotten about this little calabash. I wonder where it's been?"

"Hurray!" Little Calabash wanted to shout. "I did it!"

"For me?" Keoki asked, grinning. "Now, I can be a big kid with my own calabash!"

"See?" Little Calabash called to everyone in the kitchen. "A little calabash was big enough for a big kid after all!"

GLOSSARY

Guava: a common tropical fruit grown in many tropical and subtropical regions. It grows on trees, and, in Hawai'i, is made into many different foods, such as guava jam, guava juice, and guava frosting. It can also be eaten uncooked, as a snack or in a fruit salad.

Haupia Pudding: a sweet desert made from coconut. It is eaten for desserts at family gatherings and at luaus.

Starfruit: a tropical fruit that grows on small, bushy trees. It is similar to an apple and can be eaten raw, or used in many different kinds of desserts such as starfruit-jam-filled cookies

Mango: a tropical fruit growing on trees. It can be eaten uncooked, as a snack or in a fruit salad. In Hawai'i, it is used to make many delicious foods, such as mango cupcakes, mango bread, and mango pie.

The End